Counting Stars

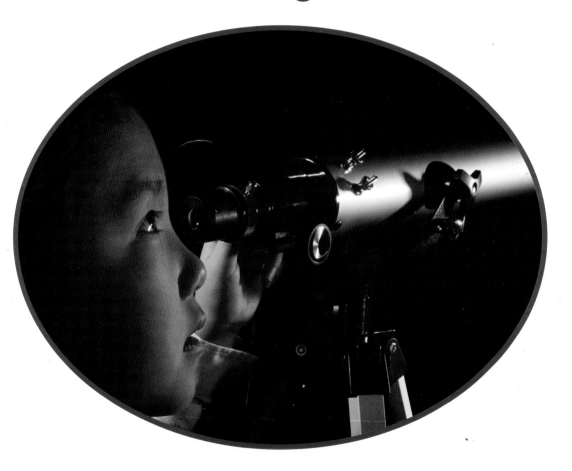

by Margie Burton, Cathy French, and Tammy Jones

You can see many stars
in the sky at night.

There are billions of stars in the sky.

Some of the stars look like they make a picture.

A group of stars that makes a picture is called a constellation. There are 88 constellations in the sky. This one is called Delphinus.

Do you see these bright stars?
They make a picture. How
many stars do you see
in the picture?

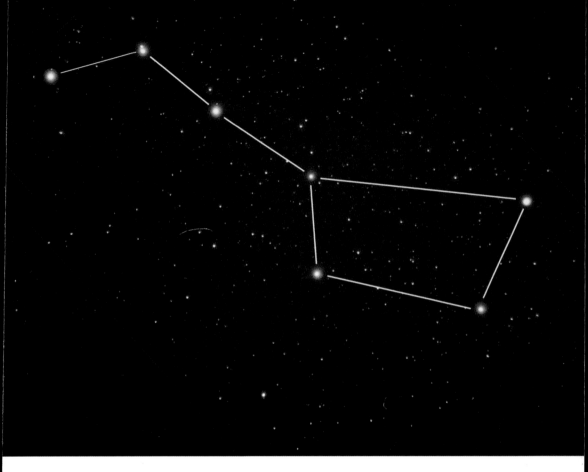

The Big Dipper is part of the constellation called the Great Bear.

In the spring, you can see these stars in the sky. They are very bright. How many stars do you see in the picture?

This constellation is called Leo. Some people think it looks like a lion.

In the summer, you can see these bright stars in the sky. How many stars do you see in the picture?

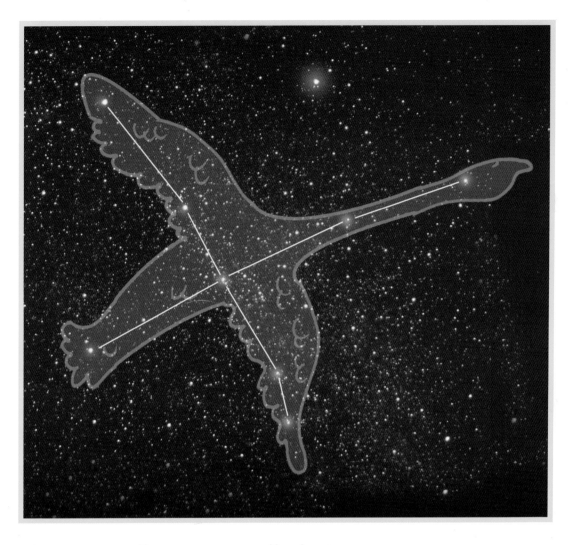

This constellation is called Cygnus.
Some people think it looks like a swan.

In the fall, you can see these stars up in the sky. How many stars do you see in the picture?

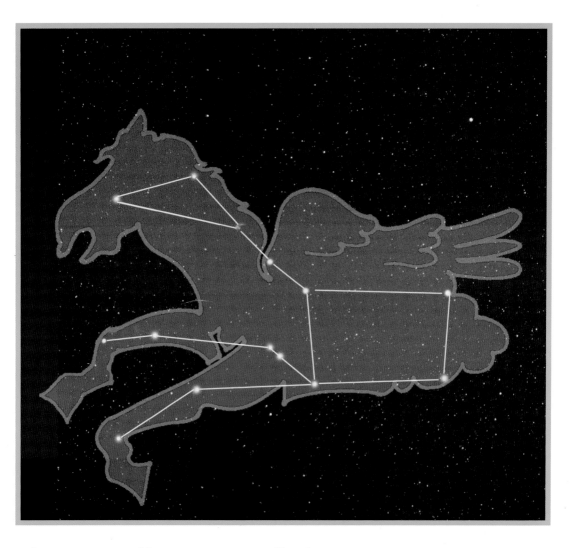

This constellation is called Pegasus.
Some people think it looks like a flying horse.

In the winter, you can see
these bright stars. How many
stars do you see in the picture?

This constellation is called Orion. Some people think it looks like a hunter. Can you find his shoulders, belt, and knees?

Look at this sky. It is made up of many, many stars. There are too many stars for you to count.

This band of light is called the Milky Way.